Little Star

This book belongs to

____

Given with love by

____

Little Star

A Christmas Gift

Bethany Beyer
Illustrated by Laetitia Zink

Paulist Press
New York / Mahwah, NJ

Cover image by Laetitia Zink
Cover and book design by Lynn Else

Library of Congress Control Number: 2024951286

ISBN 978-0-8091-6809-5 (hardcover)
ISBN 978-0-8091-8932-8 (ebook)

Published by Paulist Press
997 Macarthur Boulevard
Mahwah, NJ 07430
www.paulistpress.com

Printed and bound in the
United States of America
by Versa Press, Inc.
Peoria, Illinois
April 2025

Every night up in the sky, a thousand twinkling stars paint a picture on a dark canvas. There are many different types of stars that glimmer as the sun sets and the moon begins to glow.

Red Giants display their strength in the bright light they give off. Shooting Stars show off their speed as they dash across the sky. The Constellation Stars work together to sketch beautiful pictures. Every star has its role in the sky, and each one feels important.

Little Star did not have a role.
She was smaller than the Red Giants.
She was slower than the Shooting Stars.
She did not have a place in a constellation.
"I just wish I knew what my purpose was,"
she thought to herself. "God put me in the
sky for a reason. I need to find out
what God's plan is for me."

“Just shine brighter,” the Red Giants told her. “You will never be noticed if you don’t stand out in the sky like us.”

“Just be faster,” the Shooting Stars told her. “Watch us when we sail across the sky. Our tails leave a beautiful light behind us. Everyone is amazed when they see us.”

“Just think smarter,” the Constellations told her. “When you work together, you can make a creative picture, and everyone will remember where you are in the sky.”

Little Star felt sad. She did not feel as bright as the Red Giants, or as fast as the Shooting Stars, or as creative as the Constellations. "Why did you put me in the sky, God?" she asked. "I try so hard to be bright, fast, and smart, but I can never seem to catch up to the other stars. I wish I knew my place in your sky, Lord."

As Little Star looked down into the cold December night, she saw some figures moving slowly across the desert. A man was walking a donkey, and on it rode a woman wrapped tightly in a blanket to protect her from the cold winter air.

"I wonder where they are going. They look lost, and it is dark. I will try to help them." Little Star shined her light with all her strength. The small family still did not see her, so she tried even harder to give off a bright light in the dark sky. Finally, she saw the man stop and point up to her. He seemed to be showing his wife the little twinkle she gave off.

“It is cold, and they look tired. I am sure they want a place to rest. There is a small town ahead of them. They just need help going in the right direction.” Little Star tried to think of how she could lead them to the warmth and comfort they would find in the sleepy village. Then she remembered the long tails of the Shooting Stars as they raced across the sky.

"Maybe if I point my tail toward the peaceful village, they will find their way there." Little Star worked as hard as she could to stretch her tail like the needle of a compass, guiding the family to a safe and warm resting place. The man looked up at the sky and smiled. He continued to follow Little Star's warm glow until they reached the tiny town.

In a field nearby, several young shepherds were lying on a hill, looking up at the beautiful constellations and pointing out their favorite shapes. The smallest shepherd noticed a glimmering star with a long tail. The star was all alone, yet it seemed to stand out even more than the groups of stars that told stories with their pictures.

"Look at that star," the small shepherd said. "It seems to be calling us. Let's follow its light and see where it leads us."

The group of shepherds walked in the cold, following the shimmer of the star, until they finally reached a stable. Inside the stable, they found a man and woman nestled in the warm hay. The woman was holding a tiny baby, and she beamed as she looked down at him. The young shepherd was not sure who these people were, but at that moment he felt great joy and happiness to be in the presence of this tiny baby. He knew it was God who sent them to this place.

"Dear God," he whispered. "We saw your star. Thank you."

Little Star had never felt so proud. While not the brightest star, she gave light to those who needed it. While not the fastest, she directed those who were lost. While not part of a constellation, she had found her place in the sky.

About the Author

Bethany Beyer graduated from the University of Notre Dame and has a master's degree in special education from Syracuse University. She is a teacher in Michigan where she seeks to help diverse and nontraditional learners become successful and compassionate. She is the busy mother of four children.

About the Illustrator

Laetitia Zink is a French illustrator and author who has illustrated around fifty books, mainly for children. She has master's degrees in literature and fine arts from the Sorbonne in Paris. She lives in Paris with her three children and her husband.

Traditional Bedtime Prayers

Now I lay me down to sleep,
I pray the Lord my soul to keep.
And may God guard me through the night,
And wake me with the morning light. Amen.

I see the moon, and the moon sees me.
God bless the moon, and God bless me. Amen

Child's Evening Prayer

Author Unknown

I hear no voice, I feel no touch,
I see no glory bright;
But yet I know that God is near,
In darkness as in light.

He watches ever by my side,
And hears my whispered prayer:
The Father for His little child
Both night and day does care. Amen

Applicable Bible Verse

Isaiah 9:2, 6

The People who walked in darkness
Have seen a great light;
Those who lived in a land of deep darkness—
On them light has shined....
For a child has been born for us,
A son given to us;
authority rests upon his shoulders;
and he is named
Wonderful counsellor, Mighty God,
Everlasting Father, Prince of Peace.

Noel

An Unforgettable Night!

Claire Dumont

A charming children's book that reimagines the familiar story of Jesus's birth as if it occurred in the snowy Canadian Arctic, among the Inuit people. Ages 2-8.

6780-7 $14.95

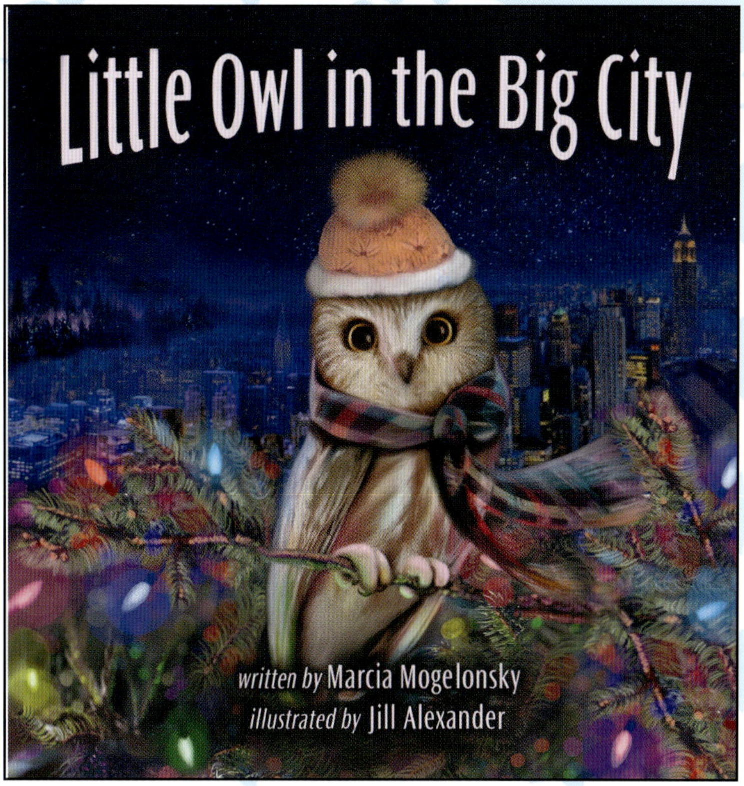

Little Owl in the Big City

Marcia Mogelonsky

Little Owl in the Big City is based on the true story of a Northern Saw-Whet owl found in the boughs of the Christmas tree at Rockefeller Center. The tree came from Oneonta, New York, 175 miles away. After being cared for at a wildlife center, the owl was released in a conifer forest in Upstate New York. Ages 7-10.

6800-2 $19.95

A Christmas Miracle

Annette Langen

Three unlikely creatures, a fox, a porcupine, and a rabbit, follow the star to the nativity, where they realize the importance of cooperation and staying together.
Ages 5-10.

6788-3 $16.95

Miracle of the Poinsettia
(Milagro de la Flor de Nochebuena)

A Retelling by Brian Cavanaugh, TOR,
with Spanish translation by Carmen Lopez-Platek

A bilingual presentation of the Mexican legend of the poinsettia. A small girl is saddened that she has no gift to give the Christ Child at the Christmas Eve procession, gathers up weeds, and finds them to be miraculously topped with glorious red flowers.
Ages 4 and up.

6687-9 $12.95